Habitats

M. J. Cosson

PERFECTION LEARNING®

Editorial Director: Susan C. Thies
Editor: Mary L. Bush
Design Director: Randy Messer
Book Design: Emily J. Greazel
Cover Design: Michael A. Aspengren

A special thanks to the following for his scientific review of the book: Paul Pistek, Instructor of Biological Sciences, North Iowa Area Community College

Image credits:
© Associated Press: pp. 15, 20; © Stuart Westermorland/CORBIS: p. 7; © Paul Edmondson: p. 9 (top); © Robert Yin/CORBIS: p. 10; © Lynda Richardson: p. 11; © Jeffrey L. Rotman/CORBIS: p. 13 (bottom); © Amos Nachoum/CORBIS: p. 19 (top)

Corel Professional Photos: cover (bottom left), pp. 2–3, 12, 16, 18, 21, 24; Digital Stock: back cover, front cover (main); MapResources: p. 6; © Perfection Learning Corporation: p. 17 (bottom); Photos.com: front cover (bottom middle, bottom right), pp. 4, 8, 9 (bottom), 13 (top), 14, 17 (top), 19 (bottom)

Text © 2006 by **Perfection Learning® Corporation**.
All rights reserved. No part of this book may be reproduced, stored in a retrieval system, or transmitted in any form or by any means, electronic, mechanical, photocopying, recording, or otherwise, without prior permission of the publisher. Printed in the United States of America.

For information, contact
Perfection Learning® Corporation
1000 North Second Avenue, P.O. Box 500
Logan, Iowa 51546-0500.
Phone: 1-800-831-4190
Fax: 1-800-543-2745
perfectionlearning.com

2 3 4 5 6 7 PP 12 11 10 09 08 07

Paperback ISBN 0-7891-6475-2
Reinforced Library Binding ISBN 0-7569-4683-2

CONTENTS

Chapter 1 The Blue Planet 4
Chapter 2 Along the Shore 8
Chapter 3 Coral Reefs 13
Chapter 4 In the Zones 17
Internet Connections and Related Reading
  for the Ocean Habitat 21
Glossary 23
Index 24

CHAPTER 1

The Blue Planet

Have you ever heard Earth called the "big blue planet"? That's because almost three-fourths of the Earth is covered with ocean water. From space, this makes the planet look blue.

The blue water of the ocean provides a home for many **organisms**. This home is called a **habitat**. A habitat has to meet all of an organism's needs. It must provide food, water, shelter, and a place for **reproduction**. Let's explore the ocean habitat.

A Salty Home

The ocean is filled with salt water. Rivers break down rocks containing salt and other minerals. When rivers flow into the ocean, they carry the salt with them. When ocean water **evaporates**, the salt is left behind. The plants and animals that live in the ocean habitat must be able to survive in a saltwater **environment**.

Inquire and Investigate
Floating in Freshwater Versus Salt Water

Question: Do objects float better in freshwater or salt water?

Answer the question: I think objects float better in _____.

Form a hypothesis: Objects float better in _____.

Test the Hypothesis

Materials
- 2 drinking glasses
- spoon
- 4 tablespoons of salt
- 2 eggs

Procedure
- Fill both glasses with tap water.
- Stir four tablespoons of salt into one glass.
- Place an egg in each glass of water.
- Observe whether the egg floats or sinks in each glass.

Observations: The egg sinks in plain tap water. The egg floats in the salt water.

Conclusions: Objects float better in salt water. The salt makes the water more dense. This means that the salt water is heavier than the freshwater. Floating is the ability of a lighter object to rest on top of a heavier object. So the heavier the water is, the easier it is to float in it.

One World Ocean

How many oceans are there? Where does one ocean begin and another end? Actually, there is just one large ocean with no beginning and no end. If you look at a world map, you'll notice that all ocean water is connected. This is why it's called the World Ocean.

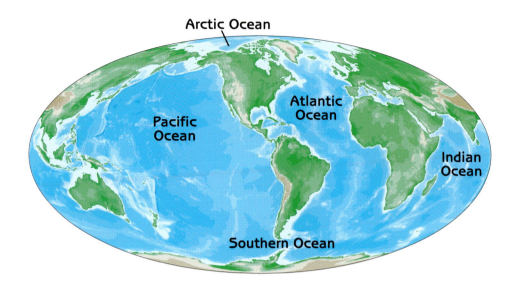

Scientists have divided the World Ocean into five smaller parts. These are the oceans you may have heard of—the Pacific Ocean, Atlantic Ocean, Indian Ocean, Arctic Ocean, and Southern Ocean. These oceans are separated by the continents.

The same salty water flows through all of the oceans. However, each one has its own special characteristics.

The Pacific Ocean has many volcanoes. It also has the deepest place on Earth—the Mariana Trench.

The Atlantic Ocean is home to the longest chain of mountains on Earth. It's called the Mid-Atlantic Ridge. Most of these mountains are underwater.

The Indian Ocean is a source of many minerals, including oil and gas. A part of this ocean known as the Red Sea contains the saltiest water on the planet.

A New Name for an Ocean

The Southern Ocean has just recently been named. It used to be part of the Pacific, Atlantic, and Indian Oceans. But over time, many scientists came to believe that the very southern part of the World Ocean has different characteristics that make it a unique habitat that deserves its own name.

The cold Arctic Ocean surrounds the North Pole. This ocean is the smallest and shallowest ocean.

The Southern Ocean surrounds the South Pole. This ocean is so cold that each year the ocean freezes along the shoreline, increasing the size of Antarctica.

Home Is Where the Ocean Is

Because the ocean is so large, it is home to millions of plants and animals. Each one is suited to life in a certain part of the ocean, such as the shore, the surface, or the ocean floor. But despite their differences, the organisms all share the same "home sweet home" in the ocean habitat.

Green sea turtles share a special relationship with ocean fish. The fish feast on algae on the turtle's shell, which keeps the shell clean for the turtle.

Chapter 2

Along the Shore

The edge, or shore, of the ocean has several types of environments. Each one is home to different plants and animals.

Rocky Cliffs and Tide Pools

Some parts of the ocean are lined by rocky **cliffs**. Seabirds often **nest** on these slopes. Albatross, frigate birds, gulls, cormorants, and petrels are just a few of these birds. Plants that grow on the cliffs must be able to tolerate the salt water that sprays on them constantly. Thrift, or sea pink, is one of the plants that covers many rocky cliffs.

Below the cliffs, **tide pools** form where rocks meet the ocean. Tide pools are areas of ocean water trapped among rocks. When the tide comes in, water rushes into the tide pools. When the tide goes out, sometimes all or most of the water in the pools goes with it. So survival in a tide pool is tough. Sometimes animals must fight not to be washed away. Other times they must wait in the dry sand or rocks for the water to return.

Time-Out! What's a Tide?

Tides are the movement of water along the ocean shore. They are caused by the gravitational pull of the Sun and Moon. During high tide, the water rushes toward the shore. During low tide, it moves back toward the ocean.

Colorful red, green, and brown plantlike organisms called *algae* or *seaweed* decorate tide pools. Green sea lettuce, brown rockweed, and red Irish moss are common tide pool seaweeds. Seaweed uses sunlight and carbon dioxide to create food. This process is called **photosynthesis**. Seaweed beds provide food and shelter for many ocean creatures.

Kelp, another kind of seaweed, can grow to 300 feet long. Colorful sponges live in kelp beds. These simple animals have small openings that allow water to flow through them, providing food and oxygen. Sea slugs feed on the sponges. Sea otters swim through kelp beds looking for sea urchins, **bivalve mollusks**, **crustaceans**, octopuses, sand fish, and squid.

Kelp

Sea otter

Food Chain Facts

A food chain is the order of who eats what in a habitat. The kelp ➡ sponge ➡ sea slug food chain is just one of millions of food chains in the ocean habitat.

Tide pools are home to gastropods. A gastropod is a soft animal that has one foot, a head with eyes, and often a round shell that grows in a spiral shape around its body. The foot of these interesting creatures is on their stomachs. That's why they're called *gastropods*, which means "stomach foot." Whelks, limpets, snails, slugs, and conches are gastropods.

Many small fish and animals have adapted to life in the tide pool. Lumpsuckers and gobies are two small fish that have developed suckers to help them hold on when the tide goes out. Sea anemones attach themselves to rocks and sometimes even to hermit crabs. Sea stars crawl slowly along the bottom of the pool. Barnacles cling to any surface where they can find food. Dogwhelks eat the barnacles.

Seals sun themselves on rocky shores along tide pools. They eat fish, squid, octopuses, and crabs by swallowing them whole.

These sea anemones catch a ride on a hermit crab.

The Sandy Beach

Sandy beaches run along many stretches of the ocean. Sand is finely ground rock, shells, and **coral** that has been carried ashore by wind, waves, and tides.

The beach near the ocean edge changes as the tides move in and out. Animals here must learn to adapt to both wet and dry conditions.

Bivalve mollusks have two hinged shells. When the tide goes out, bivalves usually close their shells and bury themselves in the sand to keep from drying out. This also protects them from predators. Mussels, clams, and oysters are bivalves.

Lugworms burrow in the sand for protection. When the tide is out, shore birds eat the worms. When the tide is in, fish feast on them.

Crabs dig homes in the sand on the open beach or in shallow water near the ocean edge. Their shells protect them from drying out when the tide is out.

Mother sea turtles crawl ashore to dig shallow holes

Loggerhead turtle hatchlings make their way to the water.

where they lay their eggs. The mothers cover the nests with sand and return to the ocean. Once the babies hatch, they crawl toward the water. Unfortunately, diving shore birds often make a meal of the baby turtles before they reach the ocean.

The area of the beach behind the **tide line** usually stays dry. Small hills of sand called *dunes* build up in this area. The dry area isn't good for most plant growth. Marram grass, however, flourishes in the sandy soil. The roots of this grass help hold the dunes in place. Sand dunes are home to birds such as plovers, oystercatchers, and sandpipers.

Salt Marshes

Salt marshes are places where land and salt water meet. Sometimes these marshes have very little water. Other times they are flooded. Marsh grasses, such as cordgrass and eelgrass, thrive in the salty water.

A variety of worms, fish, crabs, and shrimp feed on the algae and **bacteria** in salt marshes. Birds, such as herons and egrets, feast on the worms, fish, shrimp, and crabs. Fiddler crabs, snails, mussels, and oysters live among the grasses. Many insects love the moist environment of the marsh. Reptiles like turtles, snakes, and American alligators can be found in some salt marshes.

Mangrove Forests

Mangrove forests grow where river water meets ocean water. Mangroves are large trees with special roots that help them survive in salty water. Bivalves cling to mangrove roots, while crabs live in the mud under the trees. Other animals of the mangrove forest include monkeys, birds, bats, lizards, turtles, and fish.

Mangrove trees

Mud Flats

Mud flats are areas of mud, grass, and salt water that are flooded every day by the tides. Several types of **plankton** grow strong in mud flats. These organisms provide food for animals such as clams, oysters, and crabs. Mudskippers are a unique type of fish that can skip across the mud when the water is low. Tiny mud snails are another common creature found creeping across the muddy land.

Muddy Waters
Mud flats are also known as tidal flats.

Chapter 3

Coral Reefs

Coral reefs are beautiful underwater communities. Built from the shells of tiny animals, these reefs can grow huge in size and support an amazing variety of ocean creatures.

Reef Builders

Coral reefs are formed from the remains of small animals called *polyps*. Polyps live together in groups. They need warm, sunlit salt water to grow. They eat algae and plankton for energy. Polyps have protective, shell-like cups. When they die, they leave behind these hard cups. Eventually, the cups join to form coral reefs.

Builders and Decorators

There are two major kinds of coral—hard and soft. Hard corals are those that build reefs. Brain coral, hammer coral, and bubble coral are examples of hard corals. Soft corals do not form reefs. Instead, these corals provide colorful decoration for reefs. Orange tube coral, sea whips, and sea fingers are examples of soft corals.

Soft coral polyps

Reef Partners

Coral polyps share a special relationship with a type of algae called *zooxanthellae* (zoh uh zan THEL ee). The zooxanthellae live inside the polyps. They give coral their beautiful colors of pink, yellow, purple, orange, red, brown, and blue. In return, the polyps provide a protective home for the zooxanthellae. They also expose the algae to sunlight so they can make food. The zooxanthellae then help the polyps by producing oxygen, getting rid of wastes, and providing important materials for their shells.

When ocean conditions change, the zooxanthellae may leave the coral reef. When they do, they take their color with them. This is called *coral bleaching*. Coral bleaching can be caused by a change in temperature or a lack of sunlight. When the ocean conditions return to normal, the zooxanthellae return. However, if they stay away too long, the coral dies.

A coral reef habitat

Technology Link

Coral reefs provide food and shelter for 25 percent of all ocean species, so the death of coral reefs means the death of many ocean dwellers. An experiment in Bali, Indonesia, uses mild electric current to help coral grow or regrow quickly. It is called the Karang Lestari Project. *Karang Lestari* means "coral saving" in Indonesian. The project's goal is to produce coral at faster rates in order to replace coral that dies from coral bleaching and other causes. So far, the project is a success. The coral is growing more than five times faster than other coral. The increase in coral has also resulted in an increase in fish and other ocean animals that depend on the reefs.

A scuba diver examines an area of the Karang Lestari Project.

Reef Dwellers

Many ocean animals live on or near coral reefs. Larger animals such as whales, sharks, and octopuses swim in the waters near reefs. Moray eels live inside the reefs for protection. Sea turtles, crabs, lobsters, snails, and starfish crawl across the coral and surrounding ocean floor. Sponges provide shelter for animals like shrimp, crabs, and fish.

The crown-of-thorns starfish is actually an enemy of coral polyps. These starfish have 10 to 20 arms with long, poisonous spikes on them. They devour polyps, leaving only their shells behind.

Large numbers of fish swim among coral reefs. Some of these fish share special relationships with other organisms and the reef environment. For example, the parrotfish lives on the algae that coat dead coral and on the zooxanthellae inside living coral. Parrotfish peel off chunks of coral with their beaklike mouths and grind up the shell with sharp teeth. The remains of the shell pass through the fish's digestive system and become part of the sand surrounding the reef.

The clownfish and sea anemone are also reef partners. The sea anemone is poisonous to most ocean creatures, but not the clownfish. So the clownfish is able to hide from **predators** among the anemone's **tentacles**. When the sea anemone catches a meal, the clownfish eats its leftovers and cleans up.

A clownfish swims among the tentacles of a sea anemone.

Chapter 4

In the Zones

When looking at the surface of the ocean, it's hard to believe what's underneath. But below the surface lie mountains, valleys, and stretches of flat sand and mud. Some parts of the ocean are fairly shallow, while others are very deep. And while the water toward the top is brightly lit, the water near the bottom is dark and mysterious.

The sunlight, temperature, and pressure vary at different spots in the ocean. Because of this, the ocean has been divided into zones. Each zone is home to a fascinating assortment of organisms.

The Sunlit Zone

The sunlit zone is the top layer of water. It is called the *sunlit zone* because sunlight reaches the plants and animals in this zone. This makes photosynthesis possible, so algae, plankton, and green plants can make their own food. Animals can then feed on these organisms. The sunlit zone includes the shoreline and goes down about 600 feet underwater.

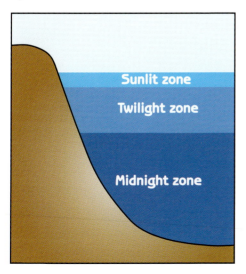

17

The sunlit zone is full of life. Large animals that live here include seals, manatees, sea otters, walruses, dugongs, whales, dolphins, and sharks. Turtles, crabs, snails, mussels, and sea anemones are just a few of the smaller creatures found in this zone. Tuna, stingrays, mackerels, and thousands of other fish swim through the sunlit waters.

The Twilight Zone

The twilight zone goes down to about 3000 feet. There's very little light in this ocean layer, so photosynthesis isn't possible. Life in this zone is dark and cold.

Some fish adapt to the lack of sunlight by making their own blinking, glowing, or flashing lights. This lighting is called *bioluminescence*. Lantern fish and hatchet fish have rows of lights along their bodies. The female anglerfish has a lighted rod above its mouth to help it find food. The viper fish has lighted lures on its body to attract **prey**.

The twilight zone is home to whales, octopuses, squid, and

Squid

Sperm whales

Sea cucumber

jellyfish. Giant squid are speedy swimmers that catch prey with their eight arms and chew it into tiny pieces. Sperm whales are square-headed whales that eat fish, squid, and octopus. Giant squid and sperm whales are deep-sea enemies that enjoy devouring each other.

The Midnight Zone

No sunlight reaches the midnight zone. The water pressure is tremendous, and the temperature is barely above freezing. No light means very little food. Most of the animals that do live here are very small and move very slowly to conserve energy. Some use smell, sound, **vibrations**, or bioluminescence to find food. Animals found in this cold, dark zone include the sea cucumber, snipe eel, opossum shrimp, vampire squid, and tripod fish.

While much of the ocean floor is muddy and lifeless, hydrothermal vents create warm homes for deep-sea creatures. These vents are pools of hot water that rise up from beneath the ocean floor. The heat and minerals from the vents provide a cozy home for huge clams, white crabs, eelpouts, and pink-skinned fish with blue eyes. Another common vent dweller is the giant tubeworm. These worms live inside hard tubes and feed on bacteria that live inside them.

Zoning In on the Ocean

The salty waters of the blue planet provide homes for organisms of all kinds. From the deepest zone to the highest rocky cliff, millions of plants and animals depend on the ocean habitat.

Scientist of Significance

Dr. Robert Ballard is an oceanographer best known for his discovery of the Titanic, a ship that sank in 1912. However, Dr. Ballard has made many other significant contributions to ocean science as well. His use of ROVs (remotely operated vehicles) to explore the oceans depths has led to an understanding of hydrothermal vents, the discovery of sunken ships, and the mapping of much of the ocean floor. Dr. Ballard's JASON Project enables students to experience ocean exploration by watching broadcasts of underwater robotic journeys.

Dr. Robert Ballard poses with JASON JR., an underwater robot used to explore the Titanic.

INTERNET CONNECTIONS AND RELATED READING FOR THE OCEAN HABITAT

Jellyfish

http://www.enchantedlearning.com/subjects/ocean/
This introduction to oceans includes maps, charts, and links to ocean animals, tides, and salt water.

http://www.mbayaq.org/lc/
Explore the ocean habitat at this Monterey Bay Aquarium site. It includes activities and live animal cams.

http://www.mos.org/oceans/
The oceans will come alive with the information you learn from this site.

http://topex-www.jpl.nasa.gov/education/cool-facts.html
This listing of "Believe It or Not" ocean facts will fascinate you.

http://nhptv.org/natureworks/nwep6.htm
Find out more about ocean communities, zones, and creatures at this Natureworks site.

http://www.enature.com/guides/select_seashore_creatures.asp
Meet a variety of sea creatures at this site, which provides basic information about hundreds of animals that make their home in the ocean.

http://www.yoto98.noaa.gov/kids.htm
Check out this student-friendly section of the National Oceanic and Atmospheric Administration. You'll find information on saving coral reefs, frequently asked fish questions, animal facts, and fun activities.

Endangered Ocean Animals by Dave Taylor. Young readers will learn about the plight of marine mammals, fish, and birds that depend on the ocean and will gain an understanding of the far-reaching effects of ocean pollution. Crabtree Publishing, 1993. [RL 4 IL 3–7] (4573501 PB 4573502 CC)

Into the Abyss: A Tour of Inner Space by Ellen Hopkins. Water covers more than 70 percent of the Earth's surface. What do we know about this part of our planet? Scientists are discovering new ways to explore this unknown water world. Perfection Learning Corporation, 2001. [RL 5 IL 4–9] (3142401 PB 3142402 CC)

The Magic School Bus on the Ocean Floor by Joanna Cole. With the help of the ever-changing bus, Ms. Frizzle turns a simple beach trip into an underwater adventure as the gang explores a coral reef, the dark ocean floor, and more. Scholastic, 1992. [RL 3 IL K–4] (4689301 PB 4689301 CC)

The Ocean Alphabet Book by Jerry Pallotta. An alphabet book of animals from the ocean with facts and information about unusual ocean creatures. Charlesbridge Press, 1986. [RL 2 IL K–3] (4141501 PB 4141502 CC)

Ocean Diving: Traveling Through Inner Space by W. Wright Robinson. From scuba diving to submersibles, this book explains how humans explore ocean depths and describes some of the sea life and dangers below the waves. Perfection Learning Corporation, 1997. [RL 3.8 IL 4–9] (4946801 PB 4946802 CC)

Oceans by Jane Hurwitz. Dive into the ocean biome, and discover the treasures found in the layers of the five oceans. Perfection Learning, 2004. [RL 4 IL 3–6] (6205801 PB)

Oceans by Neil Morris. Describes all aspects of oceans, including natural features, ocean life, conservation, and shipping. Crabtree Publishing, 1996. [RL 4 IL 2–5] (4974501 PB 4974502 CC)

Oceans by Seymour Simon. An introduction to the water that covers over 70 percent of the planet. William Morrow, 1997. [RL 3 IL K–4] (5543501 PB)

What Makes an Ocean Wave? Questions and Answers About Oceans and Ocean Life. Questions and answers provide information about various aspects of the world's oceans, waves, tides, food chains, marine creatures, coastlines, and more. Scholastic, 2001. [RL 4 IL 2–4] (6943301 PB 6943302 CC)

- RL = Reading Level
- IL = Interest Level

Perfection Learning's catalog numbers are included for your ordering convenience. PB indicates paperback. CC indicates Cover Craft.

GLOSSARY

bacteria (bak TEAR ee uh) tiny, simple organism (see separate entry for *organism*)

bivalve mollusk (BEYE valv MAHL luhsk) soft animal with two shells (oysters, mussels, clams, etc.)

cliff (klif) high, steep, rocky surface along a coastline

coral (KOR uhl) ocean animal that lives in groups and often has a hard outer skeleton

coral reef (KOR uhl reef) ridge of coral skeletons on the ocean floor

crustacean (kruh STAY shuhn) ocean animal with jointed legs, a hard outer shell, antennas, and eyes at the end of stalks (lobsters, shrimp, crabs, etc.)

environment (en VEYE er muhnt) set of conditions found in a certain area; surroundings

evaporate (ee VAP or ayt) to change from a liquid to a gas

habitat (HAB i tat) place where a plant or animal lives

nest (nest) to build a place to give birth to young

organism (OR guh niz uhm) living thing

photosynthesis (foh toh SIN thuh sis) process that uses the Sun to make food

plankton (PLANK tuhn) tiny organism that floats in a body of water (see separate entry for *organism*)

predator (PRED uh ter) animal that hunts other animals for food

prey (pray) animal that is hunted by other animals for food

reproduction (ree pruh DUK shuhn) process of making more organisms of the same kind (see separate entry for *organism*)

tentacle (TEN tuh kuhl) long, flexible body part used for holding, grasping, feeling, moving, or stinging

tide line (teyed leyen) point on a beach that tidewaters don't reach beyond

tide pool (teyed pool) area of ocean water trapped among rocks

vibration (veye BRAY shuhn) quick back-and-forth movement

INDEX

algae (seaweed), 9, 17
Arctic Ocean, 6, 7
Atlantic Ocean, 6
Ballard, Robert, 20
bioluminescence, 18, 19
coral reefs, 13–16
   coral bleaching, 14
   coral polyps, 13, 14
   hard corals, 13
   Karang Lestari Project, 15
   soft corals, 13
   zooxanthellae, 14
hydrothermal vents, 20
Indian Ocean, 6
mangrove forests, 12
marram grass, 11
mud flats, 12
ocean animals, 8, 9, 10, 11, 12, 16, 18, 19, 20
   anglerfish, 18
   bivalve mollusks, 11
   clownfish, 16
   crabs, 11
   crown-of-thorns starfish, 16
   gastropods, 10
   giant squid, 19
   hatchet fish, 18
   lantern fish, 18
   lugworms, 11
   moray eels, 16
   mud snails, 12
   mudskippers, 12
   parrotfish, 16
   sea anemones, 10, 16

ocean animals (continued)
   sea otters, 9
   sea turtles, 11
   seals, 10
   sperm whales, 19
   sponges, 9, 16
   tubeworms, 20
   viper fish, 18
ocean plants, 8, 11, 12, 17
ocean zones, 17–20
   midnight zone, 19–20
   sunlit zone, 17–18
   twilight zone, 18–19
Pacific Ocean, 6
photosynthesis, 9, 17
plankton, 12
rocky cliffs, 8
salt marshes, 12
salt water, 4, 5
sand dunes, 11
sandy beaches, 11
Southern Ocean, 6, 7
tide pools, 8–10
tides, 8
World Ocean, 5, 6

Blue-spotted stingray